by Miwa Ueda

1

Los Angeles • Tokyo • London

What is Peach Girl: Change of Heart?

Many of you have followed the adventures of Momo, Sae, Toji, and Kiley in Peach Girl volumes 1-8, published in the left-to-right format—and for that we send you a sincere "Thank you!" Peach Girl: Change of Heart is a continuation of that dramatic and cool series—only now, beginning here, it's published in TOKYOPOP's 100% Authentic Manga right-to-left format. Over the past few months, the TOKYOPOP offices have received hundreds of letters and e-mails requesting that we add Peach Girl to our 100% Authentic Manga line. Since your favorite high schooler, Momo, has a "change of heart" in this volume—finally giving her heart to Kiley instead of Toji—we thought this was a great opportunity to make the format switch. I guess you could say TOKYOPOP has had a "change of heart" ourselves—and now we are happy to present the exciting new Peach Girl: Change of Heart done the right (to left) way!

If this is your first time checking out Peach Girl, don't worry. You can catch up with the drama and excitement of Momo and her crew by simply reading the series summary and character bios on page 7. Plus, Peach Girl volumes 1-8 are still available in bookstores, so you can catch up on your Peach Girl reading anytime, anywhere.

Everyone at TOKYOPOP really hopes you enjoy Peach Girl: Change of Heart. Please feel free to e-mail any comments or questions to me at juliet@tokyopop.com.

Best wishes,

Julie Taylor
Senior Editor, Peach Girl: Change of Heart

Translator - Ray Yoshimoto
English Adaption - Jodi Bryson
Editor - Bryce P. Coleman
Retouch and Lettering - Fawn Lau
Cover Layout and Graphic Design - Anna Kernbaum

Senior Editor - Julie Taylor
Managing Editor - Jill Freshney
Production Coordinator - Antonio DePietro
Production Manager - Jennifer Miller
Art Director - Matt Alford
Editorial Director - Jeremy Ross
VP of Production - Ron Klamert
President & C.O.O. - John Parker
Publisher & C.E.O. - Stuart Levy

Email: editor@TOKYOPOP.com
Come visit us online at www.TOKYOPOP.com

TOKYOPOP Inc.
5900 Wilshire Blvd. Suite 2000
Los Angeles, CA 90036

ISBN:1-931514-19-4

First TOKYOPOP® printing: March 2003

10 9 8 7 6 5 4 3 2

Printed in the USA

上田美和
うえだみわ
ピーチガール
9

ピーチガール

MOMO vs SAE:

Death match, the whole story!!

MOMO ADACHI
With Kiley's help, she's just starting to get over Toji.

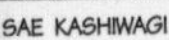

SAE KASHIWAGI
Momo's sworn enemy. Arranged to have Momo's virginity stolen. Currently dating Toji.

TOJI TOJIKAMORI
Momo's former boyfriend. Sae's mission in life. She blackmails him to dump Momo.

KILEY OKAYASU
Momo's new boyfriend. Knows Momo better than anyone. Currently in lovey-dovey mode.

GORO aka GIGOLO
Supermodel. Did he really steal Momo's virginity?

Ever since Sae blackmailed Toji to dump Momo, Kiley has been the hero "rebound" boyfriend to the heart-broken Momo. Kiley and Momo are getting along great, and Momo is finally feeling like herself again at the start of the new school year, even though she can't forget about Toji. But Sae, ever jealous of everything about Momo, enlists Kiley groupies to take part in a plot to make life hard for Momo... again. Sae and her minions lure Momo to their trap with a fake message from Toji. Then they threaten to burn her hair! Can Kiley save Momo like Toji used to? And if Kiley can save her, will that finally convince Momo that Kiley, not Toji, is truly the boy she's supposed to be with, after all?

Everything you need to know.

The more we kiss, the closer we become
Momo ...
!!
What color is your under-wear today...?

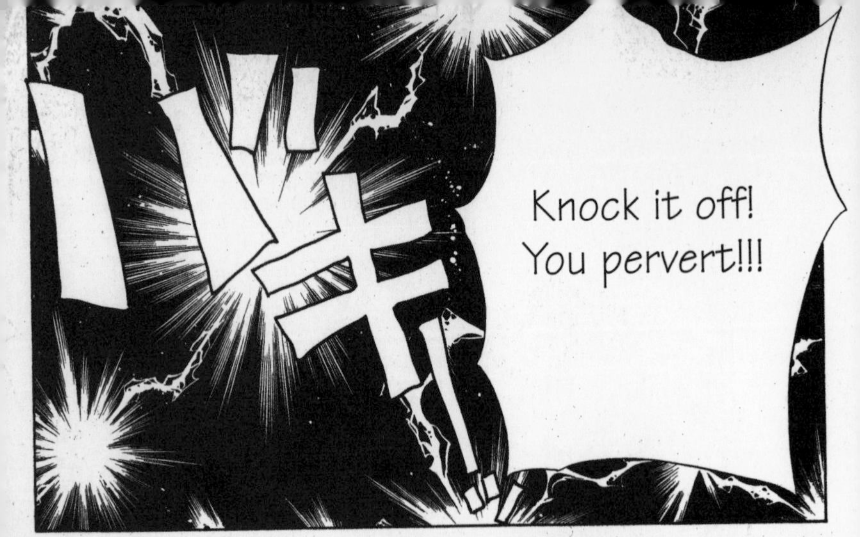
Knock it off! You pervert!!!

That's as far as it goes, buster.

Look at those two.
They're always toge-ther.
They must be dating.

I asked Momo, and she said they were just friends.
That's what she said?
But this girl said she saw them kissing.
No way!
For real!?
What's up with that?
Hmmm...

Hey, you're famous now!
You and Kiley's lip-lock action is THE hot topic around school.
....
You should probably remember to close the window next time.
Everybody can see.
But y'know, this makes it official—he's your guy.
Well anyway,
CONGRATULATIONS!!
Ah, heh heh
Uh, thanks...

……
パラ
パラ
カサ…
キーンコーン
カーンコーン
There's that slut...!
I don't believe it!

See?
What did I tell you?
....
キョロ
キョロ
....
Meet me in the yard during break.
- Toji
If it isn't the new school slut, Momo.
Waiting for someone special?
!

Too bad, swee-tie.
Toji's not coming for you... ever.
Wha...
I've been duped again!!!

You've gotta be kidding me...
Sae said so, but I didn't believe it.
But now I see it with my own eyes...
So Momo still loves Toji?
But Toji is all mine now!
Ha ha ha ha
Why are you still hung up on Toji?
Aren't you screwing Kiley now?
Hey there!
What are you girls doing!?

See ya!
ホホホ
Sae!
What are you up to!?
You don't deserve Kiley!!

NURSE'S OFFICE
I'm such a fool...

I guess a part of me is still dreaming we'll get back together.
Stupid, huh?
I was, well, I was hoping that maybe he was jealous of me and Kiley.
...to fall for such a stupid trick.
I guess I'm not over my Toji.
Meet me in the yard during break. -Toji

There's no way he'll want to talk to me now.
....
So,
when did you and Kiley start...
Hmm....
Well...
it sort of just...
hap-pened ...
heh heh
I never thought things would turn out this way.
But...

I'm glad Kiley's been there for me.
Without him, I don't think I could have made it through this.
So,
that's why...
...I have to forget Toji. For Kiley's sake, too.

Momo ...
Well ... you see...
I'm beggin' you.
Please don't tell her.
Please don't tell Momo about this. Or anybody else...
Please... don't tell a soul...

Yes ...?
I hope you're happy.

Thank you.
....
I wonder ...
Is keeping this secret from Momo really what Toji wanted?

Mpph ...
Owww! What the hell was that for!?
Are you serious about Momo?
There's a lot of gossip about you two.
But if you're not serious, then you better stop seeing her.

Oh, baby!
Are you jealous?

Do you want another reminder?
Okay, I'm sorry! Please, be COOL!
Anyway, if you really love her, just be aware that people are spreading rumors about you two.

Just remember, I personally don't approve of you dating her.
What can I say?
I'm on Toji's side.

I'm sorry.
I got tricked ...again.
Meet me in the yard during break
-Toji
So this is what those three wenches were cackling about.
I guess he heard already.
Aren't you mad...?
I'm an under-standing guy.
But if you're sorry, gimme a kiss here.
....
You could at least close your eyes.
I'm shy...
Mmm mm...

......
ドキ
ドキ
ばちっ
!!
Oh, you!
ha ha ha

あははは
パシャン
Oooh, that feels good.
Come here, Kiley.
バシャ バシャ
Uh, no thanks.
Can't you even just put your feet in the water?
Is that how bad your fear of water is?
Yeah.
Come to think of it, you almost drowned once, right?
Even at this pool, too.

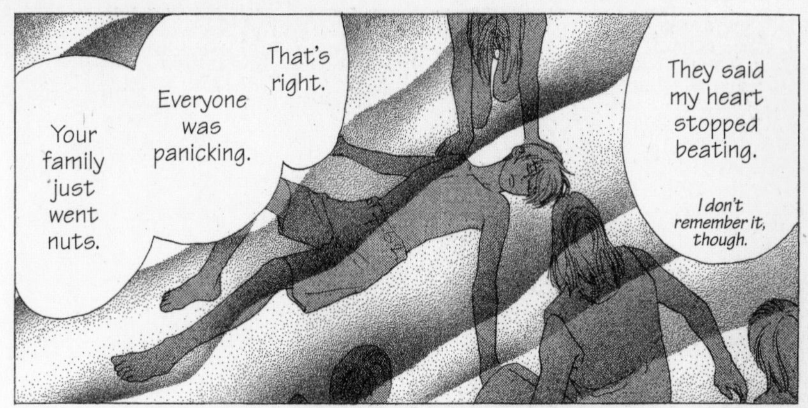
They said my heart stopped beating.
I don't remember it, though.
That's right.
Everyone was panicking.
Your family just went nuts.

So you didn't give me mouth-to-mouth?
No!
You're still hung up on that?
Damn.

Hm?

I wonder,
how did you know I rescued you?
I never told anyone.

When I first transferred here, there was a...
...rumor that you were a slut.
Someone said you even had an abortion.
That's when I first heard your name.
I sorta recalled that the girl who rescued me...
...had the same name.
The source of the rumors: Sae. ↓
Did you hear?

You knew all along?
Yeah.
You should have said something.

I'm really a shy guy,
y'know...
Eek ♡
Knock it off!
Oh, get outta here.

But it's strange, how two people meet.
If you didn't almost drown, we might never have met.
True ...
Before the accident, did you know how to swim?
Not at all.
Then why did you swim all the way out there?
The waves were really high that day because of the typhoon.

If I could swim out there, I thought maybe I could die...

Ha ha ha
I'm just kidding!
You fell for it, didn't ya!?
It's just a joke!
C'mon, I'm hungry. Let's get something to eat.
....
A joke...?
That was pretty...
heavy...

I feel
as if...
I saw a
different
side of
Kiley...

Come to
think of it,
all we talk
about is me.
I don't
know
anything
about
Kiley.

It's
not
fair...
I want
to know
more about
Kiley...
Momo.

Come with us.
Break up with Kiley.
There's no way we're giving you our blessing.
What gives you the right to say that to me?
We have always loved Kiley!
You just butted in and took over!

Everyone knows you're still in love with Toji!
It's common knowledge that you're just using Kiley to get over Toji!!
Any cute guy would have been fine, right?
You WHORE!
ピッ
What's that?
A contract for the slut.
It states that you promise never to see Kiley again.
....
And if I say no?

シュボッ
Then we give you a little makeover so you can never show your face to any guy again.
がしっ
!?
だーん
Don't worry.

We're just going to burn your hair a little.
We'll push you into the pool before your whole body lights on fire.
Your slutty face might burn a little, though.
Now WRITE.
"I will never go near Kiley again."
You think Kiley is going to fall in love with you for this? Are you that stupid?

Just write it!
チリッ
You're pathetic.
That's why Kiley could never love you.
What did you say!?
You're the pathetic one, Momo!
A user who doesn't even love a great guy like Kiley!

SHUT UP!!!!

Why would I kiss him if I didn't love him!?
Of course I love him!
If you want to burn me, go ahead!
Even if you burn off all my hair, Kiley won't care!!
You ...
You ugly...
じゅっ

That's ENOUGH! What are you wenches up to?
Kiley...!!

I thought I made myself clear… Momo is special to me.
You don't have the right to do something like this.
But Kiley!
We just...
Just GO.
Don't do anything like this again or I'll hate you.
わあっ
バタバタっ
バタバタ

フッ
Momo!
It's alright now...
カケッ
Whoa!
Aghh !
ドボーン
5

ぜは
ぜは
ぜは

I...
I thought I was gonna die...

くっ
くっ
Are you okay, Kiley?
Yeah,
but that was some good timing, babe.
Except for the ending.

When girls get jealous,
they do mean things.
I had a feeling that they were planning to pull some crap soon.
You really know everything, don't you...?
When it comes to you, just about!
We're alike, y'know.

......
I wish ...
...I could know more about you, Kiley...

はっ
Momo!!!
ざぼー
Eiyahh!

Stop it! You're getting me all wet!
I love you!
I love you...

ピーチガール

ピーチガール

Peach Club

Hello! Thanks for picking up this volume. In book 8, I got a lot of letters from people impressed with Toji, but since this book is mostly about Momo and Kiley, he hardly shows up. I get a lot of letters asking for "more Toji and Sae!" But don't worry. They'll be back, doing their thing, so just be patient!

Phew...
It's okay.
Hey, Kiley. Look...
ぺろん
Your phone case is broken.
What a drag...
Why don't you get a new one?
Well... I'm sorta broke right now.
Don't worry. I'll just tape it up.
I'm always prepared.
....

Hey!?
Why can't I knit straight?
Did I do it wrong?
Aghh! Do over!
This time I'll get it right!
Heh heh...
I wonder what he'll say when I give this to him...
Oh Momo! You made this yourself!?

Nurse! Over here!
Did you sprain your ankle?
Can you walk?
ほっ
ほっ
どっせい
Coming through!
Whoa!
cool!
Nurse Misao is really great!
Yeah,
she's like a big sis.

Owww! Big Sis!
I scraped my elbow!
Uh, Big Sis...? I have a stomach ache.
Big Sis...
They're good at nicknames.
Nurse's office cleanup crew
That's a good one.
It's perfect for her.
....
You think so?
It's like calling her "Godfather."
I'm not doing it.
Misao!
I'm done!

NURSE'S OFFICE
Mmph ...
Are you alright, Momo?
I wonder where Big Sis went?
It's okay if we just use her medicine, right?

Why don't you rest here awhile?
We'll come back to check on you.
Thanks.
Ughh...
ゴク
My period's late this month...
It usually never hurts this much...
I hate this.
If Kiley finds out I'm in bed because of PMS,
I'll never hear the end of it...

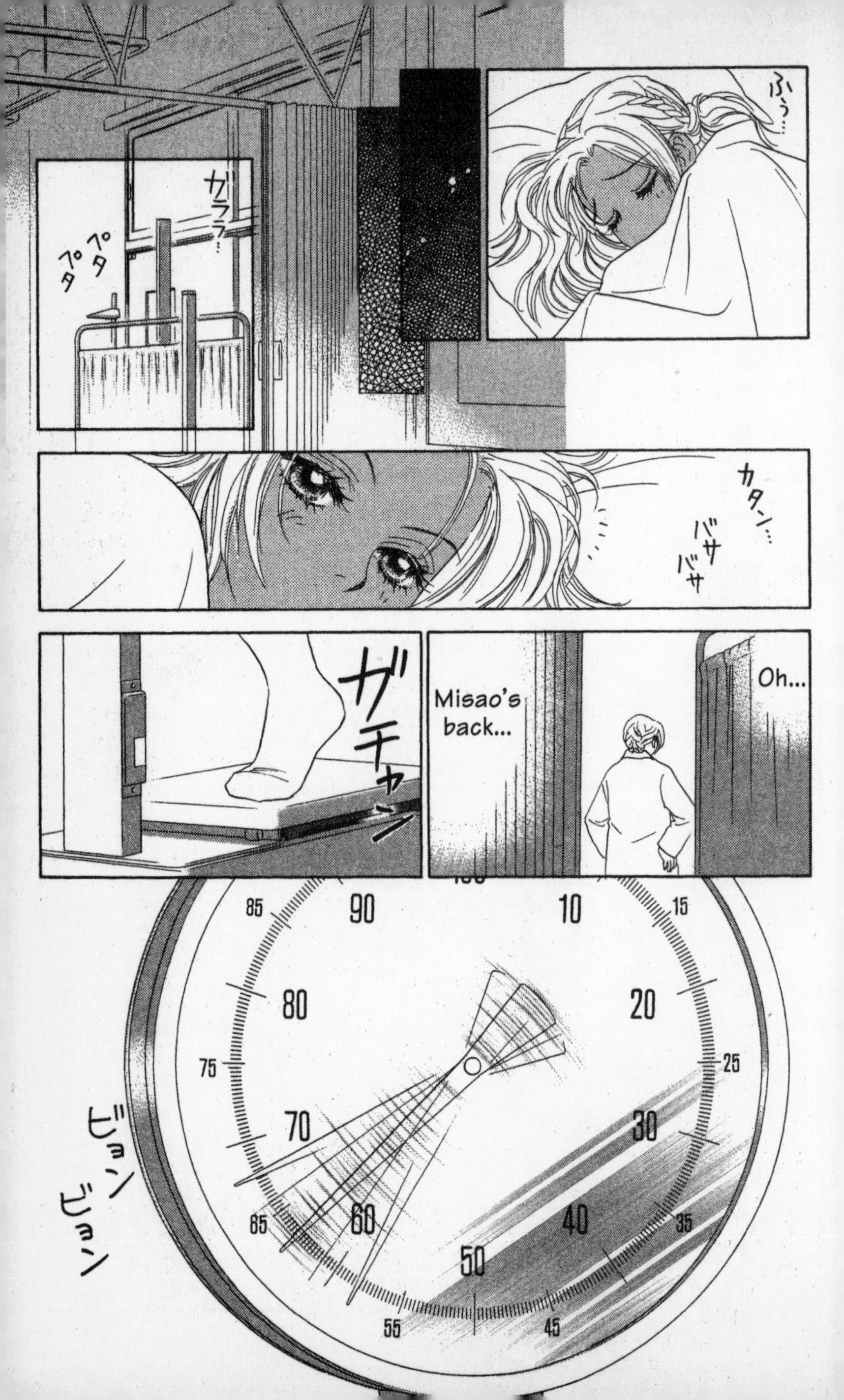
ふぅ…
ガラララ…
パタパタ
カタン…
バサバサ
Oh...
Misao's back...
ガチャン
ビョンビョン

......
はーーっ
138 pounds...
Oh... no...
Don't laugh...
Don't laugh....
Arghh! I hate my ugly, fat body!!
ぱんっ
ぱんっ

ぶはーっ
!!
Oh no...
うくっ
ぷくくくっ
I can't help it...
↰Really rude
Oh...
Momo...
You're here...?
I... I'm sorry!
I didn't mean to laugh...
Ha ha...
It's okay.

Let's just keep it a secret, okay?
あはっ
Wanna cookie?
She's mature
反省…
If it was me, I might just go nuts...
If someone laughed about something sensitive...
ガラッ
Hey!

So, you're on your period today, Momo?
This IS a girl's comic!
ブチ
Witch!
ブチ
Sadist!
Hmph!
Misao's Mini Vocabulary Primer
Period = That Time of Month
What are you drinking?
Herbal tea.
Can I have a sip?
Hey hey!
Where do you think you are?
Knock off all that frisky stuff!

I'm not being frisky.
I'm just snugglin'!
ゴロ
ゴロ
Did you forget what I said to you last time?
What are you talking about?
Who me?
Eeeeek!
I'm sorry! I'm sorry!

キラッ

Wow. That's a cute necklace.
Huh?
Oh... This...?
I never see you wearing jewelry.
It's a baby pearl, isn't it?
Like a pearl of sweat on swine.

Wha...? Why would you say that!?
It doesn't look good on her.
Kiley!
Apologize to her!
Why don't you just throw it away!?
He dumped you. So get over it already!

ガラッ
ピシャン

Kiley!

Why did you say that to her?
So, is your PMS over now?
Kiley.
We're swimming in PE anyway,
so why don't you rest some more?
Kiley!

Do you know some-thing ...
... about that neck-lace?
My bro-ther.
Huh ?
My brother gave it to her.

And she was my tutor in junior high.
Did Misao know your older brother?
They were college class-mates.
What ...?
She was...!? I never knew that!
I never told anybody.
Why did you hide it?
I wasn't hiding it.

You just weren't interested in knowing anything about me.
キーン
コーン
カーン
See ya.
NURSE'S OFFICE
That guy...

I don't know what his problem is.
He always gets like that when it comes to his brother.
He has a chip on his shoulder.
When I first met him,
he was even more out of control.
Out of control?
I think it was because Kiley was always being compared to his brother.
I guess he just rebelled. He started smoking, drinking,
and staying out late.
I think he ran away a few times, too.

He even skipped some school. Finally, his parents started hiring tutors for him.
But everyone eventually gave up on the guy.
Then his brother heard that I was studying to be a counselor,
so he asked me to help.
What is Kiley's brother like?
A very special guy.
Very kind and sensitive.
He was a great student, and very talented. He could do everything.

It makes you wonder how a guy could be so perfect.
And, of course,
he was popular with girls, so I never had a chance.
He dumped you. So get over it already!
Misao ...
Do you still love him...?
....
I... I'm sorry!
I didn't mean to...
It's okay.
Kiley's bad habits are rubbing off on me

But... I had a broken heart... until recently.
I know what it's like to not be over someone you once loved.
But I wonder why...
...Kiley didn't tell me anything about it.
That's so wild that you two have known each other for so long.
I knew you guys seemed friendly, but...
I thought he had told you, too...
バタバタバタ
Big Sis!

Waahhh! I hit this kid with a ball and he won't get up!
Help us!
Where did you hit him?
In the head!?
I'm sorry! I've gotta go!
This way!
バタバタバタ
ふう…

Momo's sewing kit

I really don't know anything about Kiley.
I wonder what kind of guy his brother is...
I remember he had a gold credit card.
It's my bro's!
I really don't know anything about Kiley.
わー
きゃー
バシャ
バシャ
......

チーララ リラリララ
ピッ
Hello.
Hey, it's me.
What is it, bro? I'm in school.
Oh yeah.
Sorry.
Can you get a message to Misao?
I wanted to change our meeting to 8 tonight.
What are you meeting about?
We're having a reunion.
Tell her I'm looking forward to ...seeing her.

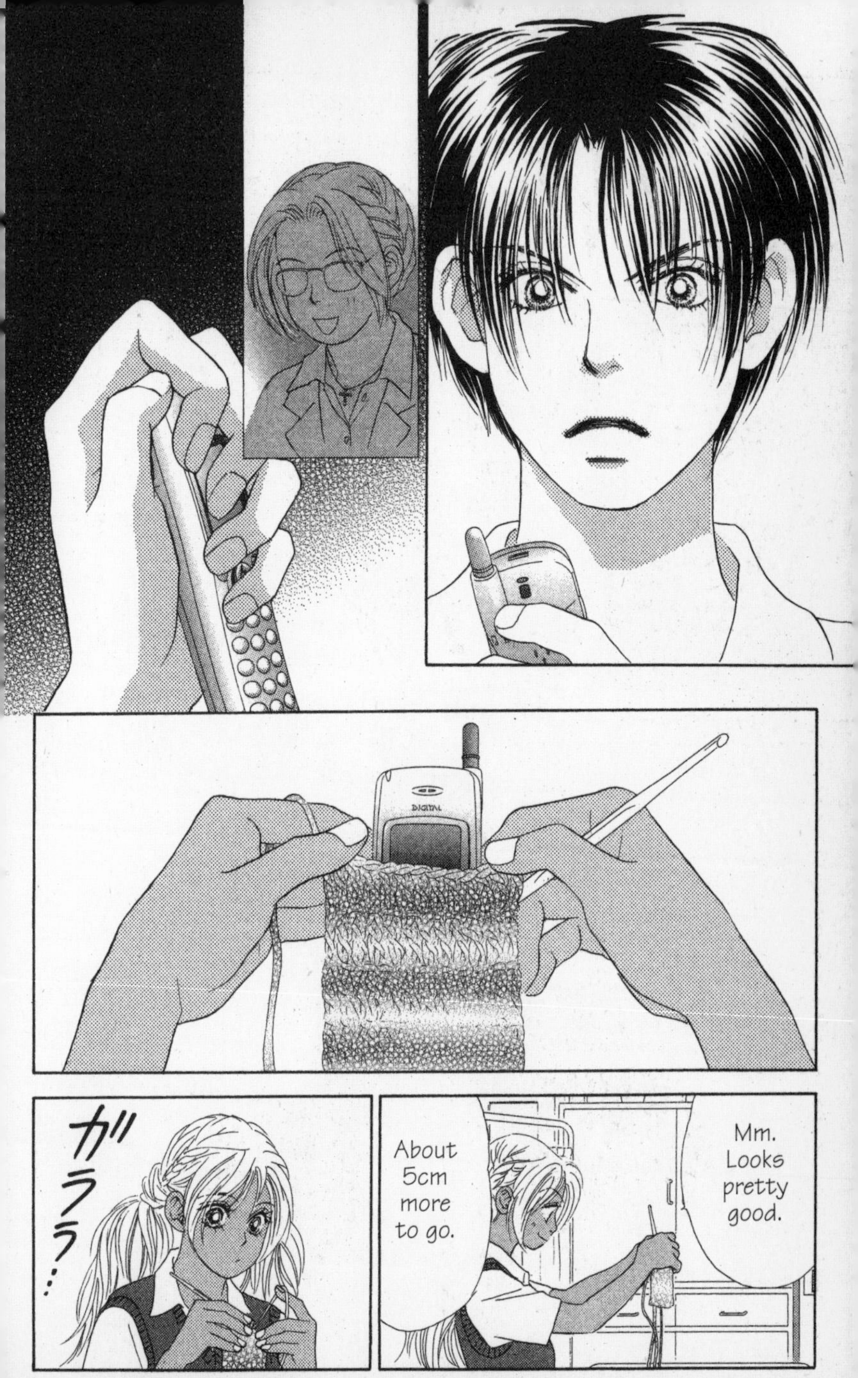
DIGITAL
Mm. Looks pretty good.
About 5cm more to go.
ガララ…

Oh, she's back.
Oh, no!!!
バババ
シャッ
!!!
!!
Oh...
Hello.
What are you doing here?
......
Where is Misao?

I think she's out in the yard.
Somebody got hit in the head with a ball.
She should be back soon.

I see.

How old is your brother?
25.
So he's a lot older.
What does he do?

ギシッ
Uh oh...

Huh?
......

Oh, uh...

I think he makes video games.
Really?
What kind of games?
I don't know.
I don't care, either
キュ
キュ
キュ
キュッ
キュッ

Wh...
What?
ばふっ
Hey, not here! What if somebody...?
ドサッ
!

Hey...
You can't, Kiley...
I'm on my period.
And it's too soon for us!

ぐぐっ…

No...
Don't...
Please...
It's not... funny...
St...
Stoppppp !!!

ドキャ

You little...!
You're worse than an animal!!
Are you alright, Momo!?
Uh...
Yeah.
Thanks ...

Come here, you!
Wait here. I'll be right back!
ガラッ
ピシャッ
That was scary...

I thought I could get out of it like usual...
I couldn't move...
But he held me so hard...
Student Handbook
Student Handbook
Student Handbook
?
Student Handbook

Is this...
Kiley...?
And who is this girl...
It's worn out, so I can't really tell...

Wow. That's a cute necklace.
!!

Wait a minute...
Is this...
Misao...?

Why does Kiley have a picture of Misao...?

Peach Club

Thanks to you, our home page at http://www.yomogi.sakura.ne.jp/~peach/ is doing well. I'm updating it as much as I can without sacrificing my work on the comic books. What really surprised me was all the letters I received from overseas—Taiwan, Korea, Singapore, America, etc. Some of the postings were "mojibake,"* so I couldn't read them, but I was really happy to see that manga can touch so many people in the world. And all this from home, too. What a century we live in!

*mojibake - unintelligible gibberish on a computer screen

What were you thinking!?
You were forcing yourself on her!
That kind of behavior is why I'm against you dating Momo!
Have you forgotten the pain she's suffered!?
Do you want her to have a breakdown and develop a fear of men!?
I swear ...

Anyway ...
If you really care about her, you should treat her better.
Under-stand!?
Why do you keep checking the time?
ぎくっ
I have plans today...
What about work?
I'm taking off early.
If you go,
I just might force myself on Momo again.

Don't mess with me, punk!!
It's in tatters...
But he's kept this photo for so long...
What does it mean...?
What if...?
ガラッ
はっ

Well?
どん
I'm sorry!
I promise not to be insensitive and do stupid things anymore!!

Uh...
Hmm...
Okay ...
It's kinda embarassing, y'know
Well, I let him have it.
But he's always in trouble, so if he acts up again, just let me know.

Do NOT pull that crap again!
I hear you!

It can't be...
It must be all in my head...

Oh, Kiley, You dropped this.
Student Handbook
ばっ

Did you...
... look inside ...!?
No.
What was that reaction?
You got dirty pictures inside?
Shut up! Don't you have somewhere to go?

What's going on?
Was I not supposed to see that picture?

I thought Misao was just your tutor?

If you've got nothing to hide, then why can't you be up front about it?

Or is it...

"I want to learn something more important..."

PRIVATE LESSONS

No way! It can't be!

There's no way Misao would do that!

I always do this.
I blow everything out of proportion.
はーっ
I should have just asked.
Like, "what's that?"
....
Should I call him...
Oh yeah.
I still need more yarn for his cell phone case.
Since I kept screwing up
メモリ手芸
Memory Yardage

I'm going to ask him tomorrow.
It all might be nothing anyway.
Oh, I'm sorry.
No prob-lem.
どん
ポテ

Kiley...!!
?
What's he looking at...?

What's wrong, Momo?
PMS again?
どよん…
ジト
はァーーっ…
ジト
ジト

I never saw that look...
on Kiley's face before...

I couldn't even say hello to him...

Hold it!!
You lied to me!
I didn't lie! I just forgot!
I waited for three whole hours!!
Help! Momo! Help me!
Outta my way, Momo! I need to slug him!
Grrr
Go ahead.

I don't believe it! You sold me out!? We were so intimate yesterday!
What!?

LIAR!!!
ドゴォ

!!

Wow!
Double punch!
おぉ…
パチパチ
Wonder twins!
They could be a dynamic duo!
They're really alike, don't you think?
You're right! They are!

Oh, come on!
That's an insult to Momo.
It's not so much your looks that are similar,
y'know?
Its more like your personalities, your attitudes.
We're alike...?
Me and Misao...?
Well, now that you mention it...

oww
I don't think so.
Are we...?
Yeah, they are!
They both have short fuses.
......
Is that why...?

はァ〜い
OK, enough talk. Finish cleaning up.

I'm sorry, Momo.
But that kid really burns me up!
Did Kiley do something to you?
You said he lied to you...

Oh that?
Well, lemme tell you ...
I had a mini reunion with some college buddies,
and Kiley didn't tell me that they changed the get-together time.
So Kiley,
I mean his brother,
left a message with Kiley for me...

How lame is that?
Because of him, I waited for three hours.
What...?
Why...?
......
He could have told her if he wanted to...
Was Kiley's brother at that reunion?
Huh?
Yeah...

He didn't want them to meet...
Is that why you wore that necklace...?
Because of Kiley's brother...
But I took it off at the last minute.
I didn't want to seem like I was still hung up on him.

Why don't you just throw it away!?
He dumped you. So get over it already!
Because Kiley said that...?
Where's Misao?
I think she's out in the yard.
She should be back soon.
I see.
What if...

He did that to keep Misao from leaving...?
Maybe he has feelings for her...

きゅっ
Wait a minute ...!!
What?
What is it?
Hey!
It's raining!
What's going on, Momo?
Where are we going?
ばしゃ
ばしゃ
ばしゃ
......

I don't want to believe it...
But if it's true, then everything makes sense.
バシャ
バシャ
ピタッ
Momo...?
Please.
Tell me the truth.

Kiley, are you in love with someone else?
....

So, you saw the picture...
You don't have to worry.
It's ancient history.
I was gonna throw it away, anyway.
くしゃ
See?
Now we're fine.

……
But you can't throw away your feelings.
You still...
She...
What are you talking about?
You're the only one for me!
……

I think ...
...you're avoiding the issue.
Why would I ?
I'm not avoiding anything.

That kiss had no feeling.
Oh, come on....
Tell me the truth!
I think you love Misao.
I remind you of Misao. That's why you're dating me, right?

I always had this funny feeling.
Whenever Toji and I had problems, you were always there for me.
But when it was good between us, you just pulled away.
But now I know. Now I know why you were always so caring.
It was because you already had someone else.
It's because you never truly loved me!!

……
ブォオ…

!
キキーッ
Kiley!?

It IS you!
You've really changed!
You're such a cutie now!
?
Who are you?

Oh,
you're so mean.
......!!!

You can't even remember your old girlfriend?

The necklace...
Is she the one in the picture...?

Peach Club

Hi again. We won't be having a "Do You Know Someone Like Sae?" corner in this volume. I'm sorry for those readers who I know were looking forward to it, but I really think that the recent letters were too similar to the last round, and in my opinion the concept has pretty much run its course. So for now, I think we're done with it. If I feel I've got stuff I've gotta write about, though, I may resurrect it. So anyway, that's all for now. I'll see you next time. Bye!

じーー…っ
ムニュッ
!!?
Morika ...!?

ピカッ
ガラガラ
Eiyy-ahhh!
ゴロゴロゴロ
ドザーーッ
Oh my God! That was close!
Scar-ryyy!!

ブォォ
You don't have to drive us.
It's nothing. I needed to go by the school anyway.
ぶすっ
Why are you sitting up front!?
Bad vibes coming from behind
↑ Forced him to sit up front
↑ Forced to sit up front

You've really changed. I didn't recognize you at first.
Ha ha.
Well, I was fat when you and I dated.
ぱん
ぱん

So she's the one in the picture...
....
チラッ

BITCH!!
キキッ
Here we are.
Be courteous.
Thank you.
ガチャッ
Oh, wait Kiley.
What?
Hmmm...
バタン
!
ブォー

Wha...?

What are you doing!?
Oh man, Momo!
No worries! No worries!

Knock it off!
きゃははは

ガラッ
Hey, Momo.
Where were you?
Hey, where's Kiley?
I got ditched.
Huh?

By who?
......

By his ex!
ぷにっ
Don't get mad.

Just take me back.
Oh, you're so cold.
It was such an emotional reunion.
Don't you have something to do?
じっ
You've turned into a major hottie!
I shouldn't have dumped you three years ago.
Look...
I missed you.

I came here to see you.
......
You were really sweet to me when we were together.
I went through a lot after that...
but I never met anyone as ...sweet as you.
I don't know why I left you.
Then why are you wearing that necklace?

Ah...
My brother gave that to you, right?
He gives presents to every girl he likes.
Kiley...
ピリリッ
ピリリリ
Wait,
I've got a call.
ずいっ☆
Is that your cell phone case?
It's all raggedy.
I don't have the cash to buy a new one.
カチ
カチ

New Message
[00/
[To Kiley
[Drop dead!
-END-
This is bad...
Was it that girl?
Is she your girl-friend?
What's that about?
ずーん
I'll walk back.
Wha...?
Hey, wait! Kiley!

ガラ・・・・ン
ぴしゃ
ぴしゃ
ぴしゃ
2-3
ガラッ
……
くしゃっ
Whaaa!!

Oh... you're here.
ドッキドッキ
You scared me.
Heh ... Were you waiting for me?
プン
ボスッ
Ow!
Wait Momo!
I'm sorry!

That girl...
The one from the picture ...?
....
It wasn't Misao...
Where were you all this time?
Look, NOTHING happened!
You don't have to worry about anything!!

......
She's pretty ...
How old is she?
Umm ... 21... I think.
Oh, so that's your type, is it?
チクリ
チクリ
...
Well, good for you, stud.
It looks like she still has the hots for you.
Maybe you can get back together again?
......
Momo...

You're the only one for me, Momo.
......
I'm sorry.
That was mean.
It was never serious between me and Morika.
But the breakup was kind of bad, so I've been hung up on it.

What do you mean?
I lost her to my brother.
But I realized something today.
I wasn't hung up about Morika.
It was because I was mad at my brother.
So you have nothing to worry about.
Really ...?
Yes, really.
Don't lie to me, okay?

ポン
ポン
When did I fall so much in love with Kiley...?
I'm OK.
Kiley would never hurt me.
He never has.

I'll believe
in him...
He's the
only one for
me now...

Wow!
You're almost finished!
When are you gonna give it to him?
I should be done by tomorrow.
It's cute!
I like the colors!
Blue's nice.
I want one, too!
You wanna borrow this book?
Do-It-Yourself Knitting
......

Hey,
could you get Kiley for me?
バタバタバタバタ
ガラッ
Kiley!!
He's taking out the garbage.
He got called down to the teachers' office.
Kiley? He just left.

Jeez! Where is that guy!?
Momo's in trouble!

Are you just naturally tan?

I'm on the swim team.
Oh really?
Hmm...

You're so lucky. I can never get a tan.
I just get red.
My skin is so delicate.

Besides, if you tan too much,
it just leads to wrinkles and age spots.
And then there's skin cancer...

And I guess you'd better watch what you eat, since metabolism slows down with age.
バギッ
バギッ
Well, see ya.
I'm used to this from all that crap Sae gave me.
Y'know ...
Kiley has a little scar next to his belly button.
I gave that to him.
hee hee
I just thought there was an ashtray there.
And then all hell broke loose.

A scar next to his bellybutton...?
....
Oh, don't tell me.
You haven't seen it yet?
You've gotta be kidding me!
How long have you been dating?
Two months!
That... That jerk...!
"It was never serious."
Finally,→ she gets it.
He slept with her!!
Two months and you still haven't got naked!?
I can't believe Kiley would wait that long!

So what?
If I wanted,
I could see it anytime.

But that's how much he cares for me.
I think.
......

Morika!!
What are you doing here?
Well,
I just wanted to finish our little chat.
We have nothing to talk about.
Go home.
And don't come back.

Wha...
What?
Let's go, Momo.
おーっ
パチ
パチ
パチ
ぎゅっ
....

チョキ
チョキ
プチン
I did it! It's finished !!!
わんわんわん
Yay!
I just have to wrap it!

I can't wait to give it to him!

8 o'clock...
......

Where are you going?
To the store.
わん わん

わん

The cellular phone you are trying to reach is out of range or has been turned off...
What?

Darn it... I came out to see him...

......

Just in case, I'll try him at home...
カチ カチ

ガチャ
RRRR...
Hello?
!
Oh, you're home!
Why did you turn your cell phone off?
Anyway, I have something I wanted to give you. Can we meet somewhere?
I'm outside right now.
Oh, did you want to speak to Kiley?
Huh?
Hello, I'm Kiley's brother.
Wha...?
I goofed!!!
I... I'm sorry!
Your voice sounded just like his, so...
I'm sorry!!
ha ha
It's alright...

Kiley left five minutes ago. He went to the bookstore by the train station.
Well, that was embar-rassing!
は〜っ
He sounded like a really nice guy.
Oh, okay ...
Thank you.
Bookstore, huh?
......
......

新刊書籍 雑誌
二宮ブックス
New Books/Magazines
NINOMIYA BOOKS
本
本
新刊
書籍
雑誌
二宮ブックス
Well, let's go!!

ガシャン
That took 30 minutes...
I hope he's still here.
キョロ…
There he is!

Here we go!
I'll surprise him.
ばっ
相撲
8
特集「川島」
I don't believe it...
Why...?

I'm in love.
Please, just once...
相撲
8
特集「川島」
...just once is all I ask.
I'll be waiting tomorrow at the City Hotel. Room 507.
What!?
She just doesn't get it, does she?
Dammit!
Just tell her off, Kiley!!

Fine. I'll do it.
Really!? Oh, that makes me so happy!
Wha ...?
Stop it. Not here.
夏場所展望号
2XXX Aug 8

ガサ
Oh yeah. This is for you.
ガサ
A present for you!
What is it?
Just open it!

Oh,
WOW!!
Your old one was getting ragged.
How much was it?
Wasn't this expensive?
Hey, a belt clip, too!
Don't worry about it.
Really?
Well then, thanks...

Momo ...!?
I HATE you!!
ばしっ

To Be Continued

COMING SOON IN

Momo and Kiley have a bigtime bond, but other people are trying their hardest to break it. Morika is after Kiley, and will seemingly do (or say) anything to get him. Meanwhile, Kiley's brother, Ryo, tries to lure Momo to a party in an attempt to seduce her by appealing to her sensitive side. Will Momo and Kiley give in to temptation, or will their love conquer all the obstacles?

Find out in

Peach Girl: Change of Heart 2,

Available Now!

STOP!

This is the back of the book.
You wouldn't want to spoil a great ending!

This book is printed "manga-style," in the authentic Japanese right-to-left format. Since none of the artwork has been flipped or altered, readers get to experience the story just as the creator intended. You've been asking for it, so TOKYOPOP® delivered: authentic, hot-off-the-press, and far more fun!

DIRECTIONS

If this is your first time reading manga-style, here's a quick guide to help you understand how it works.

It's easy... just start in the top right panel and follow the numbers. Have fun, and look for more 100% authentic manga from TOKYOPOP®!